© 2018 Timi Adeyemo. A

Published by IngramSpark

ISBN: 978-1-9996294-0-3

The Process

It is not just about the Destination…

It is about the <u>Journey</u>

TIMI ADEYEMO

I dedicate this book,

To those who are in the process

To those who believe in the process

*To those who are in motion to becoming the best
version of themselves*

I encourage you; trust the process!

Table of Contents

Introduction

What is the Process?

Process –

A series of actions or steps taken in order to achieve a particular end

A natural series of changes

When I think of the word process, I often associate it with being a means to an end. From the first definition, process can be summarized as the actions or steps taken to reach a desired end. For example, if I was to drive to see friends, driving would be the process I had to use to arrive at my destination.

Key words which stood out for me in the definition are 'actions' and 'steps'. This means the process involves movement. It requires you taking action, it requires mental and physical involvement before one can reach their destination.

Why the Process?

By starting off with the definition of what process is, it enables us to understand what it means. The first step to get anywhere in life is through obtaining knowledge and understanding.

The process is an analogy for the journey we are all on called life. The truth is, a lot of us are not happy with the lives we live. We feel there is nothing we can do to change the life we have and rather than seek change, we accept the limitations of our mind and continue to be average and strive for nothing more.

The process aims to break that cycle for those who want to progress in life. Those who are tired of the cycle of mediocrity. Those who want to break generational trends and patterns and want to become the very best they can be.

In my younger years, I was very average. I thought and believed I was not the best at anything, I was not the fastest, the strongest and definitely not the smartest. In secondary school, the friends I surrounded myself with did not help my mind-set. I had a 'it is what it is' attitude towards life. You would be surprised as to how many teenagers, youths, and even adults have this mind-set. Change is inside us all and there is a process to understanding and implementing change. The process of change will get us from where we are now to the life we have always desired. Embrace the process!

Chapter One:

The Stages of Life

There is a time for everything.

A time to be born, a time to die.

A time to speak and a time to listen.

A time to laugh and a time to cry.

 Ecclesiastes 3:1

A time to be born

I think it is best for you to get to know a little about me. I was born into a Christian middle-class family and lived the first 10 years of my life in Nigeria – I have to admit, life was good. I was born April 1997 in Lagos, Nigeria through Caesarean section. The reason for this was my head was too big to come out the natural way. Quite a humorous story when I tell others and in addition to this, I am constantly being reminded by my mother.

There is a process to being born. For you to have been born, your parents came together. The sperm meets the egg and life begins at conception. After conception, the journey from an embryo to a baby begins. The process of pregnancy is divided into three stages; first trimester (weeks 1-12), second trimester (weeks 13-27) and the third trimester (weeks 28-40).

First Trimester (weeks 1-12)

In this period, the woman will experience and adjust to a lot of hormonal changes and symptoms such as morning sickness, tiredness, and heartburn. All these changes are the process of the body getting ready to accommodate another human life. Without these symptoms and hormonal changes, a woman would not be able to carry a child.

Eight weeks into pregnancy and sections of the embryo begin to develop, such as the heart and lungs, and by the twelfth week, bones and muscles begin to grow.

Second Trimester (weeks 13-27)

Symptoms, such as vomiting, generally improve and other hormonal changes become easier to cope with at this stage. The baby bump becomes visible and the woman gains more pregnancy weight. The baby is now a foetus and will become more active in the woman's body. Between these months, the woman will feel the foetus kick and move.

Third Trimester (weeks 28-40)

The final trimester is the final stretch of pregnancy before the foetus is ready to be born. At this stage, the woman's body will begin to prepare for the arrival of the child. There will be considerably more pain around the hip and pelvis area and the woman may have trouble sleeping (all mothers deserve a round of applause).

The foetus, at this stage, should be able to survive the outside world. The foetus would have gained weight, be able to respond to light and sound and would now begin to get into the right position in the woman's pelvis ready to be born.

Pregnancy, for most women, is an amazing journey which takes their body through the process of change. I used this to illustrate what the process of becoming the best version of yourself may feel like. Many times, we may not like the change we are going through. Sometimes, we may be in pain, it may be uncomfortable, but the end product (the child) makes it all worth it. My mum always reminds me of the joy she had after she gave birth to me and although she was in pain and she had to go through a Caesarean section, it was all worth it at the end. Life is like that sometimes, we have to go through pain and hardship to get what we really want. Working on yourself will not always be easy, but it will be worth it.

Teenage Years

Being a 90s baby, means I fall into a generation category known as millennials. Millennials are those born between the years 1985 and 1998 and are perceived to be more confident, assertive, entitled, and on the flipside, more anxious and miserable than other generations.[1] The unrivalled expectation from previous generations, such as parents, has inevitably put a lot of pressure on millennials. This pressure has been a factor for many millennials when growing up.

Being a teenager/youth in this modern age is quite different from any other generation before. The expectations are much higher, but the reality is millennials so far have been a let-down generation. A generation which has been let-down by their parents; with fathers walking out on families, mothers not being able to run a household, earn a living, and having to play both parent roles in a home. It is of no surprise why this trend of being a let-down is being passed on. It is true, one can only give what they have and if all they are accustomed to is disappointments, that is all they will be able to give.

A teenager is classified as an individual who is within the age group of 13-19. Teenage years can be divided into two groups; Young teens (13-15) and late teens (16-19) however, I will adapt a holistic perspective on teenagers in this chapter.

Being a teenager in this generation can be a very confusing stage of life. It is a time where most teenagers find themselves, fit into friendship groups, and develop individual personalities. Personally, this was a time where I got to know more about myself through observing and from this I started to develop an idea of what I wanted in life. I would be lying to you if I said that I knew I would be writing this book when I was 18. If someone told me when I was 16 that one day I would write and publish a book, I would have laughed in disbelief, but here I am writing a book to guide you on what it takes to be the best version of yourself.

The teenage years is a stage where, as a parent, you don't have as much influence over your children as you did when they were adolescents. Teenagers are now being influenced by their friends more in this generation than in any other. Statistics by Parent Further state that only 10% of teenagers surveyed, said they have not been influenced by peer pressure. This means a whopping 90% of teenagers surveyed are aware they are being influenced by peer pressure.

As a disclaimer, I believe the phrase *peer pressure* has been given a negative connotation, but peer pressure does not always have to be negative, there are instances where peer pressure can have a positive impact. There is the old proverb which says; *birds of the same feathers flock together,* which is why I believe peer pressure can be used for good. Good peer pressure means a teenage child can be compelled to want to be the smartest in his or her class because their peers are doing really well. Human nature makes us naturally competitive, so this will make them strive to do what is necessary to be the smartest. That is what I call positive peer pressure, however, this is rare and, in this generation, teenagers often get it wrong.

This is not a book to tell you how bad you have it or how much you have messed up. This is a book, which from my experiences, acknowledges that it is OKAY TO MESS UP. I certainly have messed up. In my teenage years, I was focused on getting approval from my friends and I was more focused on impressing them than I was on my education and this was all due to peer pressure.

Applying the process to teenagers

Emotional intelligence, amongst other definitions, can be defined as the ability to regulate one's moods and keep distress from swamping the ability to think.[2] Better said, emotional intelligence is the ability to process and understand one's emotions at that present time. The process of being a teenager begins with understanding and applying emotional intelligence to your lives.

Using the context of secondary school, Dr. David Hamburg; a psychiatrist and president of the Carnegie Corporation says a child will get their sense of self-worth depending on his or her ability to achieve in school. A child who fails in school, sets in motion self-defeating attitudes, which can affect their prospects for the rest of their lives. At the start of this chapter, I mentioned how during my secondary school years, I had a, 'it is what it is' mindset and through this I could see some truth in Hamburg's observation. I had developed the mindset of being average because I was not the best at anything in school. So, I was not able to recognize my self-worth which led me to be prone to peer pressure. I believed I was average and this reflected in how I carried myself and the people I associated with. Are you easily peer-pressured?

The millennial generation has placed so much emphasis on education that we have allowed education to shape our identity. We have been led to believe that because we do not get top marks in mathematics or science we cannot amount to anything in life. The pressure is immense and this has crippled the ambitions of many in this generation. Your self-worth should not be intertwined with education but with your core values; what you believe deep down about yourself. The famous quote by the late Nelson Mandela says; *Education is the most powerful weapon which you can use to change the world* and I believe in education but not just the singular type of school education that has been enforced through government institutions worldwide.

Not everyone is to be an academic. In this generation, I believe we are getting it wrong by thinking academic education is the only type of education. What happened to learning a trade? Why can't you start a business? Why can't you go into fine arts? There is nothing stopping you from doing whatever you want to do in this life and the best time to adopt this mindset is in your teenage and youth years. Once past that stage, change is still possible but it becomes difficult after many years stuck in your ways with a certain mindset.

The process to realizing that you can be whoever you want to be starts with not putting your self-worth in academic education. This comes by adopting emotional intelligence techniques such as being self-aware; this is the ability to recognize your strengths and weakness. Knowing these attributes will help direct you in life and to do this you have to be able to observe. Ask yourself questions;

What do I like?

What interests me?

How do I learn best?

These types of questions will help trigger the mind and will invoke deep thoughts, which will help you on your journey to self-discovery.

Another technique to adopt is the ability to manage your emotions. Going through the teenage and youth stages means we experience emotions we have never felt before. Puberty is a time of extraordinary change in your ability to think, brain functionality, and biology (male and female). To manage your emotions, you have to be able to label and process your emotions. Questions I ask myself to help me process my emotions are:

How am I feeling? (Label it e.g. sad, happy, confused)

Why am I feeling this way? (Identify the cause)

What can I do to stop feeling this way? (Solution)

By asking myself these three questions, I have been able to process my emotions to know why I am feeling the way I am and what I can do to change it. Identifying feelings and being able to differentiate them is a key emotional skill that is not being taught in schools, and I believe should! An emotionally aware teenager will be less likely to be peer pressured into doing something they do not want to do – e.g. drugs – because they will be able to identify how doing drugs will make them feel.

In the stages of life, your teenage and youth years are a time where you should set yourself up for life. The actions and decisions you make in your youth will determine the type of life you live. It is imperative we get a head start unto the right path of this journey called life.

Chapter Two:

Delayed Gratification – Good things come to those who wait

The Marshmallow Test

Let's take a trip back to when you were four-years old. Someone proposes that they will give you a marshmallow (or any other desirable treat) but you cannot eat it until they are back from the place they went to get you another one (no time constraints). If you eat the one marshmallow they gave you while they're gone, that will be all you get. On the other hand, if you can wait till they are back, you will receive another marshmallow and will have two marshmallows to eat.

The choice is easy right? Wait for the person to come back so you can have two instead of one? If only.

Search 'The Marshmallow Test' on YouTube and be amazed as to how kids react to the test.

This test was conducted in a preschool on the Stanford University Campus during the 1960s by Walter Mischel, a psychologist. The test was to be used as a microcosm to illustrate the battle between impulse and restraint, which he believed could roughly predict where a person will end up in life. In the test conducted by Mischel, some four-year-olds were able to wait. And to help themselves wait, they covered their eyes, talked to themselves, whilst others sang as a distraction. About a

11

third failed this test and gave in to their impulse.[3] Further on to his study, he observed the same set of four-year-old kids growing up as adolescents and teenagers. He found that those who had resisted eating the one marshmallow grew up to be more confident, self-reliant and were still able to delay gratification to pursue their goals. The third who gave in to the temptation and ate the one marshmallow had fewer of these qualities. They were more likely to be upset by frustrations, be prone to jealousy and were still unable to put off their impulse and need for instant gratification.

Delayed Gratification

Gratification can be defined as the pleasure gained from the fulfilment of a desire. Delay can be defined as a period of time which something is postponed. Therefore, delayed gratification is the pleasure gained from the postponing of a desire for a period of time with hopes it will eventually be fulfilled and bring a greater reward. To simplify, it is putting off what you want now for something better at a later time.

The ability to delay gratification is critical for a successful life. This is a concept that many millennials have not grasped. We all want it now and cannot see past our impulse. It so happens that the culture of today supports instant gratification. We can see this in our everyday lives such as opting for next day deliveries, get rich quick schemes, and ordering a taxi instead of waiting for the bus. Evidence to show we are becoming increasingly impatient.

Impatience is costly. Statistics show that impatience is costing about £2000 a year according to the Financial Services Compensation Scheme. It highlights that more than half of people polled, admitted to spending more than they need for products and services because they were not willing to wait.[4] When surveyed, 92% shared the belief that society, as a whole, is becoming more impatient. 'Busy lifestyles' and 'technology' were the excuses given for the rise in impatience.

Impatience is the antagonist of delayed gratification. To become the person you want to be and live the life you want to live, you have to overcome your impulses, impatience, and put off what you want now in hope that the reward will be greater at a later time.

To simplify the concept of delayed gratification, I will explain it in the concept of education; GCSE, which is the General Certificate of Secondary Education. An academic qualification taken by pupils in secondary education in England, Wales and Northern Ireland. It covers several subjects such as mathematics, English and science. I left secondary school with 3As, 5Bs, and a C; and I have to say, I was immensely proud of myself. I would not have achieved those grades if I did not have some knowledge of what delayed gratification was. I didn't know the term 'gratification' but I understood the concept. I knew that as a teenager, education was not ranked high in my list of priorities. I did not want to be indoors in the summer while my mates were out having fun but I also knew that having fun instead of reading for exams would not be profitable to my future ambitions. I had to make a choice. I chose delaying the impulse to go out and have fun to study with the hope that after finishing my exams, I would be able to relax knowing that I did what was required to perform well in my exams. With this delay in desire (gratification), I was able to get good grades in my GCSE exams.

To be able to apply this to all areas of your life, understanding the concept of delayed gratification will help. As I highlighted in the previous chapter, the key to success is attaining knowledge, understanding it, and then applying it. Can I apply this to my 9-5 job?

Delayed Gratification at Work

In the work place, delayed gratification can be applied to the process of working your way up. The idea of promotion is very exciting to us all and we forget there is a process to it. Simon Sinek, the author of 'Start With Why', talks about why the millennial generation are not fulfilling their potential in the workplace. He says millennials have been promised so much in terms of potential that they expect everything to come to them without having to put adequate effort in. Our generation focuses more on promoting itself than on what it takes to be promoted. People skills are very important but we are too preoccupied with ourselves that we fail to show an interest in our colleagues lives nor are we willing to help when called upon. These skills are what earn promotions not potential.

Sinek highlights how impatience is detrimental to our generation. He told a story about a millennial who was getting frustrated at his work place because he saw no progress after only six months on the job. Six months?! This is why millennials are so frustrated. The solution to getting rid of frustration and getting promoted is ultimately down to our people skills or interpersonal skills as Dale Carnegie would say. We have to put off our immediate desire to have a high-paying job and focus on what will inevitably get us promoted; our people skills.

How can I improve my people skills?

- Ask questions – This shows you are interested in other people's lives.

- Listen to people attentively – You make them feel important and if someone knows they can confide in you, you are in their good books

- Do not criticize people – Criticism does not help you make friends but will lead to the other party becoming defensive. A defensive person is as good as your enemy. Appreciate people and pay them compliments.

Process and Purpose

'What is my purpose?' I asked myself many times. We, the millennial generation, have become so endowed in finding our purpose that we have neglected the process to fulfilling our purpose. The Oxford Dictionary describes purpose as the reason for which something is done or created. From that definition, the phrase which stood out to me was 'the reason'. What is your reason? Why do you do what you do? Asking yourself these questions is a good start to discovering your purpose.

I believe that your purpose is not something to be found but it finds you, IF you focus on becoming the best version of yourself. You cannot get one without the other. To become the best version of yourself, you have to go through the process.

To illustrate, let's look at an everyday item we all use; a wooden desk. The purpose of a desk is to give us a platform that can be used for various activities such as office work. However, the desk in its natural state is a log of wood. It took the thought process of man to identify the need for a desk, find a use for a log of wood and turn it into the finished product – a desk. The purpose of a desk was only achieved when the log of wood had been chopped and refined into the right size and angles to meet the requirement of a desk.

You cannot fulfil your purpose without the process. We all want the desk (our purpose) but we do not want to chop and refine (the process) the log of wood (our bad character, laziness and attitude problems).

A lot of books have been written about purpose and what it takes to find your purpose. I did some research on Amazon and looked up how many books I could find that have been written and published about purpose. The search returned with over 50,000 books. I did the same on books about the process to being the best you and it returned with over 2000 books – this speaks volumes. Too much emphasis is being placed on our purpose but we have limited guidance on what it takes to get there.

If you really want to live a fulfilled life, you cannot escape the process. Even Jesus had to go through the process. The Bible says he started ministering at the age of 30 and was crucified at the age of 33. That is 30 years of preparation and three years of purpose and now His legacy still stands 2000 years after His death.

It will take some time. That house you're working overtime to get? It'll take some time. That target weight you are slaving for in the gym? It'll take some time. Those exams you're studying for? It'll take some time. To get to where you want to be, it will take some time. This is what I had to keep telling myself when I was going through the process of writing this book. There is no such thing as overnight success. I had to put hours into research, putting my ideas together, editing and writing the manuscript. If I had not done that, there would be no book.

There is the famous saying 'Rome was not built in a day', which can be applied to all areas of your life; your relationship, work life, family, everything! Good things take time.

I read a thought-provoking quote by Hal Elrod in his book, 'The Miracle Morning', which he reiterated why there can be no purpose without going through the process:

'Know that wherever you are in your life right now is both temporary and exactly where you're supposed to be. You have arrived at this moment to learn what you must learn so that you can become the person you need to be to create everything you've ever wanted for your life'.

Chapter Three:

Follow Your Passion?

If I received £1 for every time I heard a speech urging me to follow my passion, truth is, I would not be writing this book. I would be on my private island in the Caribbean with everything I could ever need at my disposal. If you were to ask your friend or someone close to you on advice for direction in life, it is very likely you will hear something along the lines of 'follow your passion' and 'do what makes you happy'. These things are good because passion and happiness are huge factors to living a successful life, however, passion is not the only thing needed in the process of becoming the best version of yourself.

How many times have you been passionate about something and months down the line you realize you are not as passionate as you once were? Quite a few times? The reason why this happens is because our passions are based on our emotions – how we feel. According to Velleda C. Ceccoli, passion is an intense emotion, which when felt, can take control of our senses and bypass our thinking mind.[5]

Now, if our emotions are constantly changing and our passions are based on emotions, this inevitably means our passions will constantly change. One day you can wake up feeling on top of the world and the next day you're upset and confused. The same applies to our passions – you can be passionate about fashion one day and a few weeks later passionate about education. This is what to expect in life and in a verse in one of the most read books; The Bible, Matthew chapter 24:35 talks about it being a given that all things would pass away and the only being that never changes is God.

The world is constantly changing, hence why we have different seasons. Global warming is proof that the world is changing; according to NASA, the planet's average surface temperature has risen about 1.1 degrees Celsius since the late 19th century.

Personally, my passions have changed over the years. Whilst growing up and in secondary school, I was very much into rugby where I played at both club and school level. I watched, talked, and breathed rugby; extremely passionate. I got into playing rugby quite late, at the age of 13, so I was extremely motivated to improve myself to get to a good playing standard. My passion drove me to practice extra hours and it was actually during my playing days where I started realising how powerful your mind is if focused on the right things.

The hurtful truth is whilst I was playing rugby, I was never the best at my position. I had a friend who played the same position I did, and I remember he would always get picked ahead of me. He had been playing rugby longer than I had and was far more skilful than I was.

The competition between my friend and I made my passion for rugby grow. The drive to become good enough to be the first choice for my position made me rugby crazy. I went through the process of becoming a better rugby player by being committed to training, accepting constructive criticism and working on my skills consistently. This resulted in me becoming the first choice for my position in the team. There is no doubt that passion can get you results, but is it enough?

A moment to be proud of, during my playing days, was the achievement of captaining my college rugby team to a podium finish in a tournament that we finished last in the previous year. I remember when giving the team a pep-talk, I kept repeating the phrase 'right mentality' which they became familiar with as they decided to call me that phrase as a nickname!

With all these fond memories and achievements, would you believe I have not picked up a rugby ball in over three years? This is a sport I thought I would play for the rest of my life!

I was passionate about rugby until the injuries took their toll on my body and then I lost interest. Where did all the passion go? This is proof that passion is not enough to get you to where you want to be.

From my story of following my passions, you can see there are problems with this approach. A question to ask, **what are the problems with focusing only on your passion?**

By only following your passion, it suggests that is all you need to live a fulfilled and successful life. This could be in your career, health, relationships, and marriage. Passion is not all you need! **To live a fulfilled life, you need:**

1. **Integrity** – Integrity, according to the late Charles Marshall in his book, 'Shattering the Glass Slipper', is *doing the right thing when no one is watching*. Integrity is the single most important quality for success. It is the foundation value which you base your other values on. A person who lacks integrity will compromise their values when under pressure.

Millennials are being raised in a world of relativism. What is wrong to you may be right to others and many are not being brought up with universal rights or wrongs. This is why today, the culture of cheating and unfaithfulness in relationships has been hugely popularized. Why? Because many lack integrity.

Being a person of integrity means you have to live and act according to your values. Your values are your core beliefs, what you stand for. It is, therefore, very important that you define your values. To discover your values, you have to ask yourself these questions; what do I stand for? What do I believe in? What is true to me?

Many are unfaithful due to not defining their values which has led them to stand for nothing. This is, consequently, having an adverse effect on their integrity. Many of us are too soft and we compromise on our integrity when it is convenient. One who has integrity sticks to their values and what they believe in regardless of how inconvenient it may be. Are you willing to stick to your values?

2. **Commitment** – Commitment, as defined in 'The 12 Week Year', is making a conscious choice to act, in order to create a desired result. French philosopher, Jean-Paul Sartre once said, 'Commitment is an act, not a word', which means to get to where you want to be, in the process, you need to take action!

Are you committed to become the best version of yourself or are you merely interested? In 'The 12 Week Year', it highlights the difference between interests and commitments. The humorous story of the chicken and the pig at breakfast below was used to stress the differences.

'The chicken has contributed the egg and is therefore merely interested in the breakfast; the pig, however, contributes the bacon, and is thus completely committed'.

This anecdote iterates what it means to be committed. To commit to being the best you, you have to put all your efforts into developing all areas of your life. To be interested means you may only want to work on yourself at times that suit you best! When interested, you only work when comfortable. But, when you are committed, there will be no excuses. I was able to understand the concept of commitment and derive my own definition. I believe commitment is the ability to make a decision and stick to it regardless of how you feel or what your emotions are.

A personal example of when I was committed was in my gym life. In a particular season, I had an end goal of how I wanted my body to look. I realized that for me to reach that goal, I had to commit myself. I made a commitment to wake up at 5:30 am on Mondays, Wednesdays and Fridays to go to the gym. It was not an easy commitment because there were some days getting out of bed was hard, especially on the cold winter mornings BUT, I had made a commitment that regardless of how I felt (emotions) when waking up, I would go to the gym and I stuck to it. Doing this, I was able to achieve my body goals!

Humans are highly emotional beings and the millennial generation has been accused of being an emotionally unstable generation so there is no surprise as to why many struggle with commitments. If you have been struggling with being committed in areas of your life: working out, partner, faith – make a commitment to do what is right not what is easy because if it was easy, everyone would do it!

There are things to take into consideration when making commitments:

- **Have you counted the cost?** – It is very easy to make a commitment in excitement and decide to engage in something that you have not thought about the cost of. In life, there is a cost for everything. To wake up at 5:30 am to go to gym cost me sleep time and being effective in the evenings as I would end up too tired to do anything. All the same, I had counted the cost before making the commitments. Commitments require sacrifice so before deciding to commit to anything, count the cost!

- **Do you have a strong desire?** – Without a strong desire to get to where you want to be, you will struggle when the going gets tough. For you to commit to a goal, you should check to see how strongly you desire the end result. The desired end result will keep you motivated and on track during hard times.

- **Are you ready to work hard?** – Emmitt Smith, the NFL's leading all-time rusher said, 'All men were born equal, some work harder in pre-season'. This speaks volumes because apart from physical limitations, there is nothing stopping you from living a successful and fulfilled life that you once thought was elusive to you. Working hard has been over emphasized in the past fifty years and many perceive the 'work hard' phrase to be cliché. You have to be ready to put in the work required when making commitments to get to where you want to be!

It is important to note that success is not accidental and you cannot become rich or get your dream job by mistake. You have to consciously put the effort required into achieving your goals. Many millennials have embraced and adopted the 'hustle life' culture. It has been extremely glamourized over the last thirty years. This has become prevalent with the introduction of social media platforms such as Snapchat and Instagram. Many appear to portray this lifestyle of 'hustling' but the truth is they are not. These types of people are known to do things for the 'image', but in reality, it is all a façade, as many are lazy and are not ready to do what it takes. So, I urge you to not fall into the trap of self-comparison because not everything that glitters is gold. Keep doing what you do and it will soon pay off!

Hard work involves sacrifice. Sacrificing the person you are now for the one you are to become; so, in other words, delaying gratification. Hard work and delayed gratification go hand-in-hand, and by understanding and applying these two skills, the process to living a fulfilled life has just become clearer.

By focusing on your passion alone, this can limit your options and inevitably restrict your ability to get to where you want to be. To illustrate this, I am going to use the life story of one of the most innovative inventors to grace this earth; Steve Jobs. The late Steve Jobs was the Co-founder, chairman, and CEO of Apple and is known for starting the personal computer revolution in the 1970s. It is with no doubt that Steve Jobs left his mark on this earth before passing away.

Fun Fact: Did you know Steve Jobs was not initially passionate about technology? He was extremely passionate about Zen Buddhism and travelled through India in 1974 researching the religion

Steve Jobs saw the technology industry as a way to get rich. An opportunity he took when he started attending a computer club in 1975 and that was the stepping stone that led him to develop the first Apple computer.

What is that stepping stone you need? What course, class, lesson do you need to take that will push you to achieving your goals? Steve Jobs seized his opportunity to make money and as he got successful, his passion grew. If he chose to pursue Zen Buddhism alone, there would be no Apple today. Imagine a world without Apple technology?

My advice to you is to not always follow your passion but follow your opportunities! Your passion can limit your process because you are only focusing on one plan. Opportunities will always come and go but the most important is taking the right opportunity at the right time. Steve Jobs was able to grasp the right opportunity at the right time and look where it got him. Millennials are a very passionate generation but many times the down-side to passion is ignorance, which can leave you falling short in realising your full potential. Concentrating on one area alone can limit your options and if plan A fails, you should have a plan B-Z.

Proverbs 18:16 says: 'A man's gift makes a way for him'. In simple terms, what you do: your talent, career, hobby can be the propeller to the life you have always dreamt of. To do this, you have to get good at something.

You have to work on your craft because specialization will take you far. I am a firm believer that God has placed a unique gift and talent in each and every one of us but it is a shame that the culture we are in encourages people to fit in with the masses. By working on your gift and talents, this is what will bring fulfilment, purpose and contentment and will make you stand out.

Many of the world's richest people are where they are because they followed their opportunities. Jack Ma, the richest man in China and founder of Alibaba; the largest e-commerce company is a man who followed his opportunities.

After graduating from the college that he failed to get into twice, Jack faced more rejections from jobs he applied for. He was even rejected for a KFC job before he was eventually hired as an English teacher. Though, he liked his job, he was always looking for opportunities. The pivotal point in his life occurred in 1995 when on a trip to the US, he discovered an opportunity to create an internet company for China because he was not able to find Chinese products on the internet when searching. Although 1995 was the conception of his idea, two failed ventures and four years later he sought an investment to develop a site which allowed exporters to list products on the site and then, customers will be able to buy directly from China – Alibaba. By 1999, the company had raised over $25 million from the world's leading investors such as Goldman Sachs and Softbank. The icing on the cake came in 2005. Yahoo invested $1 billion in Alibaba and, through this investment, it was able to beat its main competitor; eBay as the largest e-commerce company in China.

This all started from a trip Jack Ma took to the US, which highlights that the process to living a fulfilled life can come from following your opportunities!

Chapter Four:

My First Car

I passed my driving test on the 14th of November 2014 with only three minor mistakes – I was quite impressed with myself, I must say! I passed at the young age of 17 and I was cautioned by my instructor for speeding. He warned me about my tendency to speed and he expressed his concern about how he did not want to see me back there, doing an extended driving test, because I had been banned for speeding offences. A bit stern I thought! but his advice was taken to heart and has guided me on my many travels over the years. Passing my driving test at such a young age was a blessing and a curse. My thought process right from the moment I passed my test shifted to getting my first car.

I approached my parents expressing my desire to get a car. I tried to put together a viable proposition to convince them that I needed a car. I argued that my school was reasonably far from my house and getting the bus would be more expensive. I also played the sympathy card stating how tiring it was for me having to wake up extra early just to make the bus on time, which led to me being very exhausted, which limited my learning during A-levels. This seems like a legitimate proposition, right? Well, my lovely parents didn't agree with me and their answer was, 'No, you will get a car when you turn 21'. Twenty-one?! I screamed internally. I knew I could not wait four years to get my first car, so I took matters into my own hands. I decided I would get my first car by myself.

Fast-forward a year later, I was heading to university and I still did not have a car! My university was 70 miles away, an hour and a half's drive and almost three hours by train. Not only was the time duration for the train journey longer but the price for a ticket either single or return was an extortionate amount for a student. I collated all these factors and used them as motivation to get my first car. This was September 2015 and I made a commitment and promise to myself that I would return to university in the New Year of 2016 with my car. I had four months to raise whatever amount I needed to buy a car that would not fall apart when going above 50 miles per hour!

I now had the desire, commitment, motivation and time constraint to get my first car. The combination of these four factors is important to anyone who wants to achieve anything in life. For example, you want to lose weight – the desire is already present. What you have to do is ask yourself why you want to lose weight (motivation) and that will encourage you to consistently go to the gym even when you don't feel like it (commitment). Time constraints is relative to each individual and how quick you want to see results. I had three and a half months to get my car and this was the start of the process.

Sometimes in life, you have to admit you don't know things so you can get ahead. I remember it was a Sunday afternoon after church, I grabbed my laptop and typed in 'how to make money online'. I felt quite clueless to be honest, as it was such a vague question to ask the world wide web but I did it anyway. A lot of the time, people do not start their process of growth because they are scared they will look stupid and consequently they choose not to do anything and remain stagnant. Like

Stephen Hervey says in his speech, 'Jump!' Take that leap of faith into the unknown and experience the journey to a fulfilled life.

From engaging in different activities in secondary school, I realized I had good salesman characteristics. My particular strength was being able to build relationships with different types of people and identify their needs. This observation guided me whilst I was searching for ways to make money online. I knew it would be in the service sector: me providing a service or selling a product to the end consumer. I looked at the possibilities of selling and buying on eBay, Amazon, and other online platforms. I decided eBay and Amazon would be the platform I would use to sell products as they are reputable and with an endless target market on their platform.

Having decided on the service I would be offering, I was taken aback by the biggest question yet; how would I fund buying and selling products? While I was brainstorming and debating on this business venture, I was also listening to the late Dr. Myles Munroe's series called, 'Principles To Success', where he talks about how the process of success starts by being obedient to principles. He mentioned the principle to success involved finding the seed. He uses the analogy of a tree and how God, being the creator of the earth, does not have to create another tree when one has been cut down. The principle of a tree is if you cut a tree down, you plant the seed of that tree in the right environment so it could grow. Then a thought clicked in my head and I realized I had the seed (money) to start buying and selling online. The seed was my student overdraft!

Overdraft?! Why would you use money that is not yours to make more money? This is a principle that the rich and affluent follow which makes them a lot of money. The millennial generation shares a general consensus that debt such as credit cards, loans, finance is to be frowned upon. Debt, when managed well, can help you on your way to financial freedom. An example of this method is obtaining a 0% interest rate credit card and using it to make investments; cryptocurrency, stock trading, buying assets that appreciate. Once you have made your profit, you pay back the credit card and keep your profit. Knowledge alone is not power. Knowledge and application is power and as I was able to obtain knowledge on using my overdraft to start a business, this helped to increase my financial power.

After identifying where the source of money would come from, all that was left was for me to start buying products and selling them. I approached another roadblock; what would I sell and where will I source profitable products that will not cost a fortune?

I went back to the drawing board, picked my laptop up and typed in another vague question: 'where to buy products from and sell online'. It worked! Through this I was able to find out about trending electrical products to sell on eBay. I also found out about Alibaba; the world's largest ecommerce platform where I could import electrical products such as LED glasses and speakers to sell for a good margin.

I took a leap of faith and ordered my first batch of products from China with my overdraft. It started off slow, as with anything in life, but come October, the sales started coming in. It became a weekly routine. I had deliveries coming every Friday for about three months up till the week of Christmas.

By risking my overdraft, I was able to make enough money to purchase my first car on Christmas Eve 2016. The joy was second to none! My commitment, drive, and determination had paid off. When I speak to people who tell me they have an idea they are sitting on and waiting for the right time to execute, I tell them the right time is now! The process to live the life you want is to start now! Not tomorrow, not next year...NOW! The blame is often shifted to not having enough money or time but I see those as excuses. I did not have the money to start importing goods and selling on eBay, but I was innovative in my thinking, which enabled me to get started.

There are no excuses to not live up to your potential, except the ones you make! You just have to pour your ideas (seed) out unto fertile ground where it can grow into a tree that blossoms.

Chapter Five:

What Motivates You?

The desire to get my first car poured the entrepreneurship spirit out of me and that has led me on an amazing journey to start and run multiple businesses. I realized I get a lot of my motivation from a desire to achieve what may seem impossible (i.e. my first car). Through this strong desire, it set my mind in motion to think of ways I could raise the amount needed.

I thought about getting my first car and I began to attract ways and ideas that would enable me to afford it. I started up my first business to get my first car and when the time came to change it and move on to another car, I started up my second business – a cleaning business applying the same principles as I did for the first. As you can tell, I love my cars!

The law of attraction says, 'You are a living magnet and you attract into your life the people, ideas, opportunities, and circumstances in harmony with your dominant thoughts'. You attract what you think about – if you think nothing of yourself, so you will be. If you think about being successful in life and getting rid of all self-limiting beliefs, you will become successful – as a man thinketh, so he is!

Your why?

Having migrated to the United Kingdom at the age of eleven, I was reminded countless times by my parents that my brother and I were the reasons *why* they moved

– to give us a better opportunity than what was available in our home country. Growing up, I never understood why we were being told this and often shrugged it off. When I came of age, I began to understand what they meant. My brother and I were the 'why' to their decision to migrate to England, amongst other reasons. In life, there is a 'why' for everything that exists. Why do cars exist? To provide a faster mode of transportation. Why do trees exist? To provide oxygen, wood, paper and more. Everything on this earth has a why; YOU have a why…you just have to discover it.

We millennials are facing a crisis where many have not discovered their why. The late Dr. Myles Munroe once said, 'The greatest tragedy in life is not death, but a life without a purpose (a why)'. To live a fulfilled life, you have to have a reason (why) you do what you do – it's part of the process.

'I do it for my kids'. My guess is you have heard someone somewhere say that before and you thought it was cliché? I tell you a man who does what he does to have a source of income to make sure his family does not go to bed hungry is a man with a why. Having a why is a start to living a committed life.

What is your why?

I discovered my why in my teenage years. There was a period of three and a half years where my father did not have a job. My father was the main earner in my home and having been blessed in his career with the positions he held, this period was one of the most challenging for the family.

My dad was made redundant from his job in May 2009. I was only twelve at that time and did not understand the severity of that incident. Being a man of faith, he stayed assured that it was only a matter of time before he was back working in a job of his profession. The first year went by…nothing. Second and third year…nothing! By now, there were huge financial strains on the family and we had to move houses four times in three years to manage our finances. As we were young teenagers, my parents did their best to keep the true state of our finances away from myself and my brother. However, there were times when it was hard to keep up the appearance and we were able to see how bad things were. During this time, the salary my mother got from her place of work was what we mostly had to rely on.

Over the three and a half years, my father had over fifty interviews all to no avail. It was extremely demoralizing and discouraging to see my father prepare for so many interviews. We would hope and pray it would be positive news only to hear days later that he was unsuccessful in that interview. I must say, hearing negative news so many times took its toll on the joy of the family, but as a Christian family, we believed in long suffering and knew there would be light at the end of the tunnel!

The lowest point during this period was seeing my dad in a depressed state. While my mum, having seen the state my dad was in, became extremely emotional. It is hard to see your mother cry, especially if there is nothing you can do to help. That moment, at the age of sixteen, was when I decided my family would never have go through a period like this again – and that is my why. That is why I do what I do. That is why I have read books, attended masterclasses, made investments, and started businesses. I cannot allow myself and my family to ever pass through a situation where one of us becomes so helpless due to only ever having one source of income – a job.

Putting your life and your family's happiness in the hands of one company is quite a fright and we experienced the downfall of this for three and a half years. God came through eventually and my father got a job in a well-paid company which paid him to do what he loved doing.

If you are not sure about your why, I advise you to soul search and discover the reason why you do what you do. Your why will help you to create the vision of the life you want to live. Through your vision, process comes in full effect because you have the end goal and now it's all about doing what it takes to get there.

Exercise: Write down **everything** you want to achieve on a piece of paper in no particular order – this can be education, personal, career, relationships.

Once done writing, sort these goals into categories:

Short term: These are goals you want to achieve within 3 – 6 months (e.g. read three books).

Medium term: Goals you want to achieve between 1 – 3 years (e.g. learn a new language).

Long term: Goals you want to achieve within 3 – 5 years (e.g. buy a house).

After writing these down, start to take small steps towards fulfilling your goals! Remember, Rome was not built in one day.

Your why motivates you! Through all the disappointments that life will throw at you, your why will keep you going. Dr. Zaleznik, when studying the lives of successful people, discovered the main difference between successful and unsuccessful people was in the way they responded to disappointments. My dad could have given up going on job interviews the tenth time he was rejected for jobs but no! He kept applying because he had a family to provide for and that was his why. Dr. Zaleznik highlights that life comes with disappointments and that is inevitable. What matters is how you deal with the disappointments. Did you give up on your goals because things did not work out the way you expected? Or will you take it in stride and keep pressing towards the mark?

Your journey to living a fulfilled life will come with disappointments but, your why will keep you going – *it's not how far you fall but how high you bounce that counts!*

Chapter Six:

The Power of Affirmations

It is the repetition of affirmations that leads to belief. Once that belief becomes a deep conviction, things begin to happen.

Muhammed Ali

'Do not conform to the ways of this world but be transformed by the renewal of your mind', is a popular verse from the book of Romans in the Bible. The verse continues, 'by testing you may discern what is good, acceptable and the will of God'. A biblical principle which can be applied universally to all areas of our lives. What does it mean to not conform to the ways of this world?

To not conform means to not try to fit in with others. We live in a generation where we are all trying to look the same, act the same, and possess the same things. There is nothing unique about individuals anymore. The pressure from the media to look a certain way is affecting all ages. An article published by the BBC, included the story of a young lady, aged 20, giving account of the struggles she faced trying to 'fit in'. Being a tall girl, she was picked on and this led to further insecurities about the shape of her eyebrows and the size of her forehead. She eventually changed her hair colour and stopped eating to try to fit in. This was her way of conforming to the ways of the world.

Research carried out by the All-Part Parliamentary Group on the effects of the media on body image found that:

- 60% of the public feel ashamed about the way they look

- Pressure to look good caused surgery rates to rise 20% since 2008

- Girls five and older are worrying about their looks

The turning point came when she realized it was not up to her to try to fit in but it was up to other people to stop hating her. She decided she was going to be herself and if others (the world) picked on her or not, it would not bother her anymore. Your identity cannot be formed by the opinions of others. It has to be formed by your core values and what is true to you.

What does it mean to be transformed?

The word 'transform' comes from the Greek word 'metamorphosis', which is defined as the change of the form or nature of a thing or person into a completely different one, according to the Oxford Dictionary. To illustrate, the process of metamorphosis (transforming) can be seen in the life cycle of a butterfly and how it goes through the stages: from an egg, to larva, pupa, and finally becoming an adult. Transformation is an ongoing process not a one-time event, it has to happen within you. It is very easy to change how we look on the outside but deep down have you really changed? Do you still seek the approval of others?

The verse from the book of Romans not only tells us to not conform to the ways of the world but also suggests how we can be transformed and this can be done through the 'renewing of your mind'. Bishop TD Jakes talks about how a person is a product of what they feed their mind. A racist was not born a racist but was fed hatred and prejudice – a baby was not born and instantly hated someone with a different skin colour. The baby grew up being told to perceive themselves superior to others which is what made them racist.

You cannot wake up one morning, decide to be a doctor and become one instantly. To become a doctor, you have to go to medical school, read medical books and practice to be a medical doctor. That is the only way you can go from being a university graduate to a doctor – by renewing and feeding your mind with the materials needed to get to where you're headed. The same applies to our lives, what we feed and say to ourselves is what we will become.

So, you may ask, how can I change my mindset? You can do this discovering the power in affirmations and applying it to your life. I am a strong believer that we all have the power to change our lives for the better. Before expanding on affirmations and the power behind it, I want to touch on an area which is so important to the process of living a fulfilled life but yet neglected and dismissed. This is our self-talk – the way we talk to ourselves and our outlook (perspective) on life. Let us examine the two modelled conversations below that we encounter daily.

Conversation A

Person 1: How are you doing?

Person 2: I'm not too bad and you?

Person 1: Yeah, not bad.

Conversation B

Person 1: How are you doing?

Person 2: I'm good and yourself?

Person 1: Yes, I'm good too!

What is the difference between the two brief conversations? Perspective.

Do you see a half-filled cup of water as half full or half empty?

Your perspective is formed by the way you speak to yourself; your self-talk. Conversation A depicts a person who may not believe that there is power in what they say to themselves. As James Allen writes, 'As a man thinketh so he is'! This is true because what you think about internally, reflects on the outside so if you think you're not doing 'too bad', that is what your reality will be because as a man says so he is! How you feel about yourself and what you say to yourself will become your reality. Both parties in conversation B may not have felt good about themselves at the time of that conversation but they had adopted a positive perspective unto all things. This is very important in the process to become the best version of yourself.

Brian Tracy, in his book, 'Change Your Thinking, Change Your Life', talks about self-image, self-ideal and self-esteem. All three are intertwined, and together, make up your personality. Self-ideal is made up of all your hopes, dreams and visions and is the perfect image of the person you would like to become. Self-image is how you see and think about yourself – what you imagine on the inside will reflect in your behaviour on the outside. Developing a positive self-image is a good step to being the best version of yourself. Your self-esteem is what you believe is true about yourself – how much do you like yourself?

As humans, I believe everything we do while living is to help increase our self-esteem or to protect it from being diminished by people or circumstances. A person who lacks self-esteem is one who is sensitive to the opinions of others. Like the young lady mentioned earlier, she was sensitive to what people thought of her and therefore she let the opinions of others influence how much she liked herself. Apart from the context of body image, many of us have low self-esteem issues because we have given our power to others and their opinions. Some people are too scared to start that business they've always wanted to because they are scared it will fail and, in the process, they would lose the approval of their peers. Some people are scared to go on that great life adventure because their 'friends' are not into activities like that. Are you one of those people? It is time to take your power back.

Affirmations are one of the most powerful tools to transforming your life! I first heard about the concept of affirmations in Hal Elrod's book, 'The Miracle Morning'. Through his S. A. V. E. R. S. practical technique, I realised I HAD the power to transform the way I thought and felt about myself – my self-esteem. In the process to becoming the best version of yourself, affirmations will give you the power to develop the mind-set that you need to take your life to the next level. Affirmations are a way of reprogramming your mind to focus on YOU and not what the world says about you.

Affirmations can be used positively and negatively. Think about those times you have said you cannot do something and now that thought has become a belief? Those are negative affirmations and can work against you in the process to living a fulfilled life. Many times, you find that people have settled for a specific lifestyle because they first affirmed they could not do any better and their affirmations became a reality. You do not have to be one of those people. You have the power to change what you believe and this can be done through positive affirmations. The law of subconscious activity says that whatever you repeat over and over to yourself while conscious, your subconscious mind will eventually accept it as the truth. Through positive affirmations, you can take full control of the thoughts in your mind and overcome self-limiting beliefs.

My personal experience using affirmations came when I went through a season where I was battling with self-comparison. Self-comparison is a dream killer and can make you take the blessings in your life for granted. Growing up and being surrounded by people who were not transformed in their thinking, we all shared the same beliefs and attitudes to life. There was the belief that it was okay to hurl abusive words at each other all in the name of 'banter'. Through this belief, I started believing things about myself that were not necessarily true. I compared myself to others physically, as I was not the biggest. This was an area which frustrated me because in life there are only a few things you have no control over and one of them is your size.

What self-comparison did was it stole my joy and peace. There was the constant cycle of thoughts in my mind telling me I was not enough (bear in mind, I am perfectly normal) and this halted my process to being the best version of myself. Through observation, I realized I had an inferior complexity mind-set, which is the lack of self-esteem and feelings of not measuring up to standards. Do you suffer from an inferiority complex? Here are signs you do:

1) You are ultra-sensitive – critical comments send you into a state of self-hate

2) You compare yourself to others – You focus on other people's best qualities and compare yourself to it

3) Perfectionism – You think anything you do is not good enough

4) You are secretly judgmental of other people – You judge people because you secretly covet what they have

Do you do any of the above? I did all of the above and realized it was time to take my power back. After reading, 'The Miracle Morning', I wrote a list of affirmations I would say to myself everyday immediately after waking up. I encourage you to do the same but please note that before writing your affirmations, you have to be sure what it is that you want to change. If in doubt, this may discourage you from being consistent.

The time you say your affirmations is crucial. I would recommend saying your affirmations in the morning because your mind is fresh and the brain is operating at a higher frequency than it would later on in the day. However, different affirmations can be effective at different times.

I am ENOUGH because Christ lives in me, so I cannot feel insecure, I cannot feel inferior and I CANNOT compare myself

This was the first thing I told myself as I woke up each day. I intertwined my biblical belief in this affirmation as I believe it gave me that extra push to change what I believed. I placed emphasis on the words in capitals as I was saying it. It is important to say your affirmations in a positive energetic state as that has the power to shift mind-sets.

A few of my affirmations are:

I am God and self-reliant, I do not need the approval of others

There is no scarcity in my life, I am abundant. Money and blessings are coming to me

I am determined to not think about what other people think of me

My affirmations are ever changing as I keep discovering self-limiting beliefs that need to be challenged. If you are not sure what affirmations you want to speak into your subconscious, here are a few universal affirmations that will help you shape the way see and feel about yourself:

I accept myself for who I am

I am confident in my ability to make successful decisions

I will strive to be the best that I can be

I am going to be successful, regardless of what challenges come my way

Your mind-set will not change overnight, but by affirming positively every day, eventually, there will be a shift in the way you think.

Consistency is the key to effective affirmations. Once you decide to challenge your self-limiting beliefs, you have to commit and be consistent whilst affirming. I touched earlier on what it means to make commitments in chapter three and by applying these principles to your life, you will succeed in the process of becoming the best you.

Chapter Seven:

What do you believe?

Your belief system will determine the life you live. If you believe that life is for the taking and your potential is limitless, so will it be. On the other hand, if you believe you are in this world just to get by, then so will it be. If I were to ask if you TRULY believed you could be successful and live a fulfilled life based on the daily habits you exhibit, what would your honest answer be? If yes, great! Keep doing what you do. If no, then there is work to be done.

The word 'belief' can be used interchangeably with the word 'faith'. By definition, belief is the acceptance that something exists or is true, especially without proof. While the definition of faith is having a strong belief or confidence in someone or something. In this chapter, we will look at belief systems through the perspective of faith and examine what forms our beliefs.

In the book of Hebrews, faith is defined as the substance of things hoped for, the evidence of things not seen. From the several definitions, we can see that faith involves trust, hope, acceptance and confidence. Faith, in the 21st century, has been associated mainly with theists and those who practice religion but this is not always true. According to John C. Maxwell in his book, 'Make Today Count', he highlights that we all have faith and every day we act on beliefs that have little or no evidence to back them up.

When you go to bed at night, you expect to wake up in the morning – that is faith. When getting in the car and you start the ignition, you expect the car to start – that is faith and when the sun sets in the evening, you expect it to rise the next morning – that is also faith. As humans we have the free will to believe in whatsoever we choose to and this is what really defines our belief system – what we choose to place our belief in. A theist has faith that there is a God and an atheist has faith that there is no God. Both have strong beliefs that they are right and neither can provide evidence to prove their point.

The Placebo Effect

To illustrate my point let us examine the placebo effect. The placebo effect first emerged around the 16th century as a way of researching the relationship between the mind and healing. French philosopher Michel de Montaigne wrote in 1572 on how he observed a few people who, upon the sight of medicine, felt better. The placebo effect was popularized by Henry Beecher after the second world war where he observed the correlation between the pain men suffered and their mind-set towards the pain. In his 1955 publication, 'The Powerful Placebo', he observed the psychological state of men who were badly wounded and noticed they did not request morphine as they had little pain. They were able to cope because they believed they could. Placebos are substances made to resemble drugs but are made of inactive substances such as starch or sugar. Placebo drugs are normally given to a group of people without the knowledge of the patients or the medical personnel who administered the drug. According to research carried out by the US National Institute of Health in 2004, doctors widely prescribe placebos to deflect requests for unsuitable medications.

Further research into this phenomenon by the US National Institute of Health found the placebo effect was most effective when treating pain. In a similar study conducted in 2005 to find out the effects of placebos, it was discovered that placebos stimulate the release of the body's natural painkiller opiates, which is why some people have believed a drug they were given made them feel better but really their health improved due to their belief system. The Placebo effect is proof that there is power in believing – do not underestimate the power in your belief.

If you argue for your limitations, they are yours!

'I cannot do it'.

'I will never be good enough'.

'I never have enough money'.

Are you arguing for your limitations?

As I wrote on affirmations in the previous chapter, I mainly wrote on positive affirmations. We live in a world of opposites so where positive affirmations exist, negative affirmations also exist. Negative affirmations are silent but deadly because most times, we do not realise we are affirming negative beliefs into our subconscious mind. How many times have you said one of the sentences above? Negative belief systems all start from ideas. Ideas that have been accepted as the truth. This is why I believe ideas create behaviours which form attitudes that produce results.

Let us examine a self-limiting belief of 'I can't do it'. This belief started off as an idea. For example, an aspiring entrepreneur intends on forming a start-up business with a huge potential but he made the mistake of confiding in someone who did nothing but discourage him and beat down his idea. He chooses to accept the idea of the other person as the truth and eventually gives up on that idea. The idea reinforced, influences his behaviour. Now, anytime he thinks of a business idea, he remembers the one time he failed to work on his idea because he believed he could not. This idea formed an attitude of being a failure and produced results of limited progress in the course of his life.

Do you know that limitations are not real? I have realised that with every limitation, there is a way around it. For example:

Gravity – Airplanes (Wright Brothers)

Night-time – Electricity/Light bulb (Thomas Edison)

Nature – Sea – Boat/Ship

With all the limitations listed above, there was an invention which found its way around the limitation. These inventions came about because the inventors were able to understand the limitations. This involved spending time with the limitation and finding out what was true about it and what was not. This is the same for us. Through understanding your limitations and getting to know why you think the way you do, it will help you to develop a solution to your limitations and inevitably turn it around for your good. Why can you do this? You can do this because you have a mind and your mind is your power. Your power is your mind which is why humans have been behind the greatest inventions from the beginning of time.

Get rid of all limiting beliefs today!

Returning from the little digression, I want you to ask yourself a question, **'What do I believe in?'** Take a minute to ponder on what your belief is. This could be what you believe about yourself, your faith, your ambitions or what is true to you. I cannot tell you what to believe in but I can hope that what you choose to believe in will help you in your process to living a fulfilled life.

What can you believe in?

1. A higher being – God

To believe in a higher being, i.e. God, means to acknowledge that there is a force greater than yourself. From a religious perspective, to acknowledge there is a sovereign being which you cannot see or prove exists means you are a person of faith. Eighty-four percent of the world's population has faith, according to the Washington Times and a third of them are Christians. A study conducted by the Pew Research Centre's Forum on Religion & Public Life covering more than 230 countries and territories found that nearly 9 out of 10 people identify with a religious group meaning; out of the 2010 world population of 6.9 billion, 5.8 billion believed in a higher being.

Those 5.8 billion people believe in a being that they cannot prove exists?! 'They must all be crazy!' could be the perspective of those who are not among the 5.8 billion believers. There must be a reason why that amount of people have faith! My belief in Jesus and the Bible, as a Christian, keeps me going through tough times. As much as I know it is in my hands to do what is needed to live a fulfilled life, I also know there are times when my spirit gets down and I need some motivation. During these times, I turn to the promises of God in the Bible i.e. in Isaiah 40:31 it says that 'God will renew the strength of those who put their hope in Him' – which lifts my spirit when I feel tired or out of focus. More promises are in Jeremiah 29:11 which says, 'the plans of God is to not harm me, but to prosper me and to give me hope and a future'. All these promises I use to encourage myself when things may not go as planned.

To believe in a higher being gives me reassurance that I am not in this world alone left to fight the battles of life by myself. It reassures me that in the process to get to where I want, there is a force behind me guiding and directing me to the desired destination. Does that not comfort you? That is why 5.8 billion people believe in a higher being.

Will faith help you in your process? I believe so!

2. Ideas, Dreams & Visions

I am left disappointed when I speak to people in their twenties who do not know where they want to go in life or have no plan for the course of their life. They mostly have spread themselves too thin and got involved in everything possible from music to sports to academics etc. This has prevented them from finding their measure. While there are others who are not interested in the seriousness of life at all and refuse to grow up. It is time to put away limiting beliefs and birth those ideas inside of you! It is time to build your life vision of where you want to be in a year's time, three years' time, and further on. It is time to dream big dreams!

What millennials are good at is being innovative. Seeing and doing things differently are among our strengths. Innovation means new ideas. According to Richard Branson, the founder of Virgin Group, any idea can be a great idea if you think differently, dream big and commit to seeing it realised. The book of Proverbs chapter 18:16 says 'the gift of a man will make room for him and will bring him before great men'. I believe that man can be you – male or female. What is that idea, that talent, that thing you have been working on? All those things you have been working on in secret, it is time to bring them out because when you do with diligence and integrity, it will propel you to unimaginable heights and like Proverbs says, it will bring you before great men!

I would like to urge you to believe in your ideas and dreams because this is what will be centre to your process. The process comes with doubters, those who will laugh at your ideas and those who will write you off, but I assure you, if you DREAM BIG, it will bring you before great men.

Dream big!

3. Good things coming your way; are you gripped with fear?

Fear can also be known as, false evidence appearing real and you would be amazed as to how many people settle for less, due to fear. Dr. Myles Munroe once said that 'the richest place is the graveyard because the graveyard is where most people take their dreams and ideas' as they feared doing anything out of the ordinary – they feared being great. From this I was able understand Marianne Williamson's writing on what our deepest fear is, 'Our deepest fear is not that we are inadequate. Our deepest fear is that we are powerful beyond measure. it is our light, not our darkness that most frightens us. We ask ourselves, who am I to be brilliant, gorgeous, talented, and fabulous? Actually, who are you not to be? You are a child of God. Your playing small does not serve the world'.

Whilst in the process of becoming the best version of yourself, there will be occasions where you will be faced with fear. Could it be in the scenario where you are trying to overcome social anxiety and you have been asked to give a speech at your mate's birthday? Your old social anxious self will see this as an avenue to be embarrassed but you know the process to overcoming social anxiety involves you changing your perspective and seeing this as a good thing because doing it will mean you are a step closer to overcoming your fear. In other words, there are times you will feel the fear but according to Susan Jeffers you should feel the fear and do it anyway! Fear may make you perceive speaking in public as a bad thing, but in reality, it is good because you are overcoming that fear.

Many people are stuck in the mind-set that good things are not supposed to happen to them – they have developed a negative belief system. What do you believe? Do you expect to not do well in life? If you do, it is time to fight that mind-set and face your fears. Some people sabotage any good thing that come their way because their mind-set is set up to believe otherwise.

Think about that relationship you sabotaged because you believed they would never be able to love you? Or what about the times you were given a gift but your mind-set made you reject it because you felt they would demand something in return? These scenarios are examples of how people sabotage the good things in their life. As I touched on in chapter six, positive affirmations is a method that can be used to change your mind-set, you can apply the use of affirmations and change your belief system.

From today, choose to overcome fear and start believing good things are coming your way!

Chapter Eight:

Relationships – Are you the one?

A big part to why millennials are misunderstood is due to how bad we are in our relationships. We suck at dating, we have terrible relationships with their families and we do not know how to sustain our friendships. Many have embraced the 'cutting off' culture where if a friend or partner was to do something that offends us, we would cut off all form of communication from that person. Is this what we want our generation to be known for? 'The generation that gave up on love?' Not if I can help it!

My focus will be on dating and the process to a successful dating relationship. In this chapter, I will also be highlighting the things we may be doing wrong and how we can turn our relationships around for good. In our modern-age society, there is a robust amount of focus on love, sex, and relationships and I am perplexed as to why many get it wrong.

Fun Fact: Did you know that millennials spend 10 hours a week on dating apps? Men spend an average 85 minutes per day while women spend 79 minutes on apps like Tinder.[6]

If you are not taken aback by that statistic how about this one?

Fun Fact: Did you know that in 2018, single people spent 96 million hours and £2 billion on bad dates?[7]

The research carried out by eHarmony, one of the world's largest online dating platforms, claims that 52% of dates leave singletons feeling disappointed.

Millennials and other generations are investing so much time, money, and effort only to be feel disappointed after the date. With so much focus on this area, why is it that many of us seem to get this area of our lives wrong? There are a few reasons as to why we suck at dating.

Why do we suck at dating?

The Illusion of Choice

Tinder, Facebook, Instagram, Snapchat, eHarmony, Twitter, WhatsApp…these are just a few of many social media platforms that are used by many to meet their potential partners. I believe this is a reason why many are struggling to have successful dating relationships – the variety of options. Through social media and the power of the internet, we are now able to communicate with people on the other side of the country or the world. If you take some time to observe the dating trend of the baby boomer generation (1946-1964), dating was based primarily on proximity because people did not always have the means to get in touch with those far away so, this reduced the choices in the search for a partner. Now you can set up a date with someone two hundred miles away by swiping right.

The illusion of choice mindset has been adopted by many and this has affected how we handle our relationships. We take our partners for granted because we believe there are plenty more out there so we do not put in the effort required. In the scenario where your current partner leaves you because you did not appreciate them, what do you do? You find another one the same way you found them – through social media, and the cycle repeats. Then suddenly we realise we are getting older and still alone but have no idea why?

It is time to start appreciating each and every one of your relationships, friendships, and romances. To appreciate your relationships, you have to rid yourself of the mind-set that there are other options. Doing this builds up your resilience to be able to invest time and effort into making your relationships work.

Media Influences

Millennials grew up watching Disney movies and learned about what Disney's version of love was through the stories they told. The problem is Disney's version of love only works in movies – they are incredibly inaccurate and can end up doing more harm than good. Does happily ever after exist? In movies it does, but not in reality.

The process is all about the journey to becoming the best version of yourself and living your best life. Along that journey, there will be disappointments. People will leave because they don't like the idea of you becoming a better person. There also will be days where you dislike the process but you know at the end of it all it will be worth it. This is the same as relationships, there will be ups and down, but being with the right person makes it worth it.

Due to social media, many are growing up with unrealistic expectations of what a relationship should be. Physical expectations. According to social media, if your boyfriend is not 6 feet or taller, he is to not be given a chance and for men, if your girlfriend is not a certain size and of a certain curvaceous shape, you should find someone else. You would be amazed how many people have adopted these false criteria as standards for their dating relationships. Don't get me wrong, I am not saying you should not have standards and preferences but what I am saying is you should not let the media dictate what your preferences should be.

Physical attributes do contribute to the essence of being in a loving relationship but it becomes a problem when that takes centre stage in the relationship. Meaning it becomes a problem when two people start a relationship based only on physical attraction. According to Gary Chapman, the author of the '5 Love Languages' book series, a relationship should be formed on similarities in your values, morals, spirituality, social interests, vocational visions and the desire or lack of desire to have children. The media does not focus on these aspects in a relationship, only on the physical.

You may have heard of the term 'power couple', especially on social media platforms such as Instagram. Couples labelled power couples may not necessarily be in positions of influence or may not be doing anything significant but because they 'look' the part, they are labelled a power couple. To other followers, this may leave them feeling insignificant in their relationship because, according to the media, they do not look the part, which, in worst case scenario, can make a person leave their loving relationship in search of a relationship that fits into society's standards.

Has the media made you develop unrealistic expectations in your relationships?

We Want Instant Gratification

We live in a microwave society where everything is ready at the snap of our fingers. Our culture allows us instant access to just about anything – if we want food, we have it delivered with a click of a button and when it comes to dating, Tinder offers the same service. We have taken this culture of convenience and tried to enforce it into our relationships.

We suck at dating because we date for the sake of it. Without a clear vision as to why you are investing time, money, and emotions into a person, when the relationship falters, it can leave you frustrated, alone and depressed. Many expect to find a life partner without really understanding what the term means. Like the Bible says in the book of Genesis, your partner is to be a suitable helper and you a helper unto them so if you are dating someone without the intentions of being a helper then what is the purpose of that relationship?

There is also the element of impatience, which is preventing many from having meaningful relationships. The problem is instant gratification is addictive and often becomes a habit which tends to seep into our love lives. Through primary and secondary school, a trend of everyone wanting to be in a relationship became prevalent. I put this down to our deepest human needs, which is to love and be loved. Everybody wants to love and be loved but it is a shame that everyone wants to love when they don't understand what love is or are not mature enough to love.

It is alright not to jump from relationship to relationship if you do not feel you are ready for one. The preliminary for a loving relationship is to be in touch with yourself and get to know yourself which I will touch on later in the chapter. The impatience to wait till you are ready for a relationship is killing this generation and one thing we need to realise is that love is not to be experienced in an instance, but in a lifetime – a process.

We Are Too Promiscuous

Attitudes have changed toward sex and sexuality since the 1960s. To better understand how attitudes have changed, it is best to understand the attitudes before the 60s.

Divorce was not accepted.

Women were expected to remain virgins till they got married.

If women got pregnant before marriage, they were ostracized.

The generation feared sexually transmitted diseases and infections.

The shift in attitudes began when medicine to treat STDs were developed and the pill, created by George Pincus in 1959, helped to reduce one of the biggest fears of having sex – pregnancy. The Women's movement also began where the norm was challenged about pre-marital sex. The result of this revolution meant:

Divorce rates doubled with 42% of marriages in the UK ending in divorce.

Sex has become noticeable in day-to-day media, e.g. using sex to sell products.

Dating is less about finding a life partner but more of being sexually active.

The result of the 60s revelation led to a culture of 'hook-ups' being created. Sex has been taken out of marriage and turned into a sport. Many individuals have multiple sexual partners, which does nothing for you but leaves you feeling alone. Rather than enjoying sex in the confines of marriage, sex is no longer a special or unique experience but just another 'night out.' In their bestselling book, 'The Wait,' authors Devon Franklin and his wife Meagan Good used their experience on how they waited till marriage before they had sex to encourage many. Their message is waiting, rather than rushing can be the key to finding the person you are to be with. They emphasise on how the wait gave them the power they had to be able to see each other for who they were after they put sex on the shelf. This helped them in the process to being the best version of themselves individually and also in their relationship.

Before taking on another sexual partner, think about how you felt the last time you let that guy or lady in and how empty you felt after. Sleeping around is not healthy, as it temporarily makes you happy but in the long run it takes more from you than it gives. Sexual relations can make you overlook certain behaviours/ values which do not agree with what is true to you. A few years down the line when the sexual excitement has faded, you begin to realise how both of you are not so compatible.

It is time to put emotional compatibility first, before sexual compatibility, and take back control of your relationships!

Are You The One?

'Are You The One?' is an American television reality show aired on MTV. The plot of the show involves young singles on the quest of love. They have been secretly paired into couples by producers via a *matchmaking algorithm*. The aim of the show is to see if the individuals can identify who their 'perfect match' is while living together. If they do, they all get to share a prize of up to $1 million.

To be honest, I was hooked on the show for the first few seasons because I was interested to see how science can bring people together with claims they have found peoples' perfect matches. Out of the six seasons of the show, only the participants in season five were not able to find all eleven perfect matches, which means they missed out on money. The remaining contestants from the remaining five seasons were able to identify their perfect match and therefore they should have found love, right? Wrong! I did a little research into the aftermath of all the seasons to find out which perfectly matched couple were still together. To my surprise, I was able to find only one couple, from the first season, who were a perfect match, that were still together. There were more 'no-match' couples that ended up together than perfect-match couples. This brings me to ask what happened to finding the one? Who qualifies as the one? Is there only one person for me?

I have struggled with finding answers to those questions for a long period of time. I am not sure if I have found the answers. However, in the search for answers, I have realised how much emphasis has been placed on finding 'the one'. So much emphasis on 'the one' but no light has been shed on the process required for each individual to go through to become ready for 'the one'. By focusing on finding 'the one' you take the focus off yourself and place it on someone else. So, when you find someone thinking they are 'the one', they become your source of happiness, which, according to Terry Cole Whittaker, leads to a 'relationship built on guilt, dominion, and control'.

In her book, 'What You Think of Me is None of My Business', she highlights that a loving relationship can only begin from a transformed person and a transformed person is one who accepts self-love, worthiness, and a God within. She stresses that the big secret in life is that one must unconditionally love and accept themselves in all areas of their life before getting into a relationship. In the microwave society of today, one of the reason people serial date is because they have not healed from previous relationships and experiences of life. So, they cover up and carry the hurt and pain from these previous encounters along with them. The process to a loving relationship, starts from you!

The Process Before The One

To run, you first have to walk. You cannot do one without the other and the same applies to relationships.

The most important thing you have to do before the one is to – find yourself.

The process of you finding yourself involves spending time alone with yourself but many find it hard to do because we fight being alone. We live in a society where it is very easy to be involved in many projects and we use this to hide our inability to be alone. Time alone will help you get to know yourself through deep thinking and observations. You will be able to pick up on your likes and dislikes and through this you will be able to slowly piece together characteristics you would appreciate in a partner.

I went through a season where I found myself entertaining 'potentials', as I would call them, but deep down I knew they were not the one for me. However, I struggled to break it off because I struggled with being alone. I liked the attention and the approval I got from them, which made it hard for me to be honest with myself. The cycle was I would become involved with a female, invest time, effort, and emotions into getting to know them, realise we do not have much in common and then decide to go our separate ways. The cycle kept repeating itself and the change came when I met someone I realised was the one for me, however, I could not go into a loving relationship with her because of all the baggage I was carrying from previous relationships. It was at that moment, I realised I needed to spend some time alone, get to know myself, define my values and reflect on previous experiences.

As a Christian, this was a time I was able to get closer to God and work on my faith. Being involved with others, meant I sometimes was not able to focus on my walk with God. As Matthew 6:33, says, 'I should seek first the Kingdom of God and all its righteousness; THEN, all other things will be added to me', I realised I was going through the process wrong. I put other people before my faith and beliefs, which, according to Matthew 6:33, is wrong. I should put God FIRST then other things, i.e. the one.

My time alone helped me to find myself, enjoy my company and work on my belief system.

Before the one, you have to find what it is you have been put on this earth to do. I am a firm believer that everyone alive right now is alive for a reason and it is up to each individual to discover that reason. No matter how big or small, we are all here for a reason. There is a Biblical quote which says, '*Life is God's gift to you and what you do with it is your gift back to God*'.

Some may read that quote and not agree with it because they feel that life has not treated them fairly, but I just want to remind you that out of the 6 billion humans on this earth, there is nobody exactly like you – you are unique! Nobody can think the way you do, nobody can sing the way you do, and nobody can express themselves the way you do. You are an individualised expression of God, so it is time to start cultivating your gifts, ideas, and talents.

I think many have underestimated the time and effort that needs to be put into making a relationship work and this is a reason why I believe it is best to discover or be in the process of discovering your purpose before the one. It helps you to focus and get your priorities right. It is better to walk in purpose and be single than to be in a relationship with no purpose or sense of fulfilment in life.

Remember the process to a loving relationship, starts with you!

Chapter Nine:

Marriage & Family

You have spent time alone getting to know yourself, found your purpose, worked on your craft and you are now in a loving relationship with the one. What next?

Statistics from the Office for National Statistics UK reveal that between 2002 and 2014, there was an increase in people who were divorced and a decrease in those who were married and in 2014, 1 in 8 adults in England were living as couples but not married. Why are fewer people getting married? Is marriage becoming outdated? Has our generation forgotten the importance of marriage?

Purpose of Marriage

According to the book of Genesis, which narrates the biblical account of creation, chapters one and two talk about God creating the heavens and the earth, the trees and then cultivating the land, which afterwards He was pleased with this. Throughout the whole creation story, there was only one thing God created that He considered as 'not good'. Genesis chapter 2:18 says, 'Then the Lord God said, 'It is not good for the man to be alone. I will make a suitable companion to help him.''

That was God's answer to man's deepest need. Man's deepest need is to love and be loved – union of life with another. That is why, when God made Eve, Adam expressed in verse twenty-three, 'At last, here is one of my own kind – Bone taken from my bone, and flesh from my flesh'. A very romantic story, in my opinion, and from this, Adam was able to identify just what was right for him, one of his own kind, one who he was to unite with, take as a wife and become one. That sums up the purpose of marriage – unity.

God saw that it would not be good for man (man and woman) to be alone, so he made a companion just for him. Gary Chapman the Author of, '5 Love Languages', believes that marriage is designed to be the most intimate of all human relationships. A relationship where a husband and wife are to share life intellectually, emotionally, socially, physically, and spiritually to work together to achieve the aim of becoming one. Marriage described in one word is unity. So why is it that statistics show there is a decline in those getting married and an increase in divorces? This means there is less unity in our generation!

Marriage and family did not begin with western civilisation but some evidence can be found in the earliest written records which date back to over 4000 years ago in the Code of Hammurabi. This code discusses the relationship between husbands and wives. The laws of Manu, which were written over 3000 years ago, cover the duties of husband and wife. Other notable historic figures such as Aristotle talks about marriage in his ethics while the Chinese used the concept of yin and yang to illustrate what marriage should be about – unity![8]

The purpose of marriage is unity but divorce rates are still on the rise! I believe a reason why is because many do not understand the roles in marriage.

Roles in Marriage

Marriage, depending on who you are, where you're from, and what you do can mean different things. However, the roles in marriage are quite universal. No, this is not where I am going to say the man should be the main earner of the family and the woman should be a stay-at-home mother. It's time to get rid of those ancient beliefs and embrace the 21st century. However, as much as I encourage you to embrace the 21st century, it is important not to forget the basic foundation that make marriages and families work.

To make a marriage work, I believe;

The Man is to be the Head of the Home

For a man to be the head of the home does not mean the wife is beneath him. The purpose of marriage is unity, which in other words means equality. Marriage is a partnership where a man leaves his house and joins with his wife so they can become one. Meaning as they are one, they are equal. According to the book of Ephesians chapter five, verse twenty-three, which says, 'The husband is the head of his wife as Christ is the head of the church'.

As a Christian, Jesus is the head of my faith and the one I look up to when in need of guidance. Although I have the free will to not look to Him for help, I know it is in my best interest to do so. Similarly, it should be like this in marriage where the woman can make decisions but knowing well that if she makes those decisions with the guidance of her husband, she can be rest assured she made the right decision because she made it in unity –

with her husband. This also applies if the decision did not go the way she wanted, she can be sure she's not in it alone.

In our current society, the rise of feminism has brought threat to the role of a man in the institution of marriage and family. As men, we have been brought up to lead and naturally, being the physically stronger partner, it is in our nature to provide and protect our family. This does not mean the wife cannot provide and protect but I think the key to success in a home is having clear joint conjugal roles – this is where husbands and wives share housework, childcare, decisions, and leisure time and this way the husband can fulfil his instrumental roles and the wives can fulfil their expressive roles in a state of unity.

Husbands should love their wives and wives should submit to their husbands.

One area I do believe society is taking the wrong direction on is in the role of the woman submitting to her husband. Although I don't think the word 'submit' is a user-friendly word, however, it can be defined as accepting the authority or will of another person. Once again this comes across as forceful but I think we are all missing the point here.

The purpose of marriage is unity, so how do you become one? By submitting to your spouse. Apostle Paul, when addressing this issue over two thousand years ago, knew it would be a persistent problem throughout the ages and that is why in the book of Ephesians chapter five he encourages the wife to submit to her husband and also commanded the man to love his wife. Many think the wife is to submit and that's it. To love is to submit and to submit is to love.

Ephesians 5:22 ESV 'Wives, submit to your own husbands, as to the Lord'

Ephesians 5:25 ESV 'Husbands, love your wives, as Christ loved the church and gave himself up for her'

Ephesians 5:31 ESV 'Therefore a man shall leave his father and mother and hold fast to his wife and the two shall become one flesh'

I think divorce rates are rising because many view submission as outdated and traditional. The husband and wife are no longer in unity and want to do different things, have different mind-sets, goals, interests and neither are willing to compromise. You cannot have marriage without compromise because it is the joining together of two different people with different experiences in life.

Will compromise save your marriage? Try it and see!

There must be unity between husband and wife when raising kids

Growing up, I knew my parents were in unity because many times I tried to be sly and get away with something by asking my mother, she would refer me to my dad to ensure they made a joint decision. Back then, I did not appreciate it but now I can see the importance of having a united front when raising children.

Children are very observant and pick up on your strengths and weaknesses as individual parents as well as a unit. If you, as parents, do not share the same values in bringing up your children, there may be room for exploitation.

Like Gary Chapman says in, 'The 5 Love Languages,' areas such as core values and beliefs should be talked about in depth before making the decision to get married. For example, the father may not be a devout Christian and sees no reason why the children should go to church but the mother, a devout Christian, strongly believes it is imperative that the children go to church. Sunday morning comes, and she asks her husband to help get the kids ready for church and he passes saying they do not need to go to church because he doesn't go. In a marriage like this where they do not share the same belief on a key value such as faith, there will be arguments.

Before committing and getting married, ensure you have these conversations with your fiancé as unity in core values will make the process of unity easier. If you are engaged, *startmarriagehere.com* is an easy-to-use online resource that will provide you the tools you need to help your marriage last and it gives you access to over 25 years of premarital counselling in the form of author Jeff Jelton and New York Times bestselling author Dr. Gary Chapman.

It should be formed on love

Love is patient, love is kind. It does not envy, it does not boast, it is not proud. It does not dishonour others, it is not self-seeking, it is not easily angered, it keeps no record of wrongs. Love does not delight in evil but rejoices with the truth. It always protects, always trusts, always hopes, always perseveres. According to 1

Corinthians, that is what love is. For those struggling to define love, there you go! Could not have been described any better.

If your marriage is not built on the above, then what is it built on?

Love today and see love find its way back to you.

Family

Family is the most important institution in our society. As you may have heard the saying, 'charity begins from home', so does everything else! Love, happiness, and joy begin at home and if by chance none of this exists in a family, it would be hard for the members of that family to love, be joyous and be happy. Daniel Goleman, in his book, 'Emotional Intelligence', highlights that family life is our first school for emotional learning. In the unit of the family, he says is where we learn how to feel about ourselves, how to think about our feelings and how to express our hopes and fears.

Many times, if you dig deep into the background of criminals, they had a troubled childhood. I will use the story of Edmund Kemper to illustrate this. Edmund Kemper is a 6-foot-9-inch-tall serial killer who hated women. He murdered several members of his own family and six women in California in the 1970s. Why would a man do such a thing?

At the age of nine, his parents divorced and his mother, who was an alcoholic, blamed him for the divorce. She carried out her frustration coming from a failed marriage and forced him to live in the basement, isolating him from his kin. At age 15, he was sent to live with his grandparents who then confiscated his rifle as he could not stop killing animals. In return, he murdered his grandparents shooting them to death and claimed he wanted to 'see what it felt like'.

A troubled childhood precedes a troubled life. The hate that was poured unto him by his mother led him to want to kill other women. This is why, I believe, it is very important for parents to put their differences aside and unite to raise a home full of love, emotional balance, and harmony. I have spoken to many who, out of pain, talk about how their father or mother left when they were young and the effects it had on them. They cannot trust because when they relied on their parent to show-up at an important event e.g. graduation, their parent let them down, so they carry their inability to trust into their present relationships.

When looking at a sociology study as to why there has been an increase in family diversity over the last 40 years, it highlighted a few statistics. In 1971, just 8% of households were headed by a lone parent, but by 2011, that figure had reached 22%. This correlates with the fall in two-parent families from 92% in the 70s to 78% in 2011. This means that many young people are growing up without their fathers or mothers around in some scenarios.

Successful relationships such as marriage and family all have two things in common – love and unity. If they are both present in more relationships, there will be less breakups, heartbreaks, and divorces. I go back to my point in chapter eight that it all starts with you. The process to a successful relationship, marriage, and family starts with you. By discovering yourself, understanding your partners values and sharing them in marriage, you can be sure you will not become a divorce statistic!

Chapter Ten:

The Process

Back to the question I asked at the start – what is the process? The process is understanding how things work. Not only understanding how things work but also applying it to our lives. The process is learning how to walk before you can run. The process is doing what you need to do now in order to get to where you want to be. The process is patience, faith, hard work, delayed gratification, _____, feel free to include other things you feel will guide you on your journey to becoming the best version of yourself.

There Is No Overnight Success

Internet sensation, Michael Dappah, otherwise known as Big Shaq, took the internet by storm in 2017 with his unorthodox novelty song 'Mans Not Hot'. As you can guess by the title of his song, he clearly was not hot! The song saw huge commercial success, peaking at number one on iTunes Christmas Day in 2017. It peaked at number three on the UK singles official charts, charted in over fifteen countries and was certified gold in the UK, which means it had over 400,000 sales and streams combined. The YouTube video alone gained over 250 million views!

'Who is Michael Dappah?' you may ask, 'And why was he successful overnight?' Michael Dappah is an English rapper, actor, and comedian who is known for portraying the fictional rapper Big Shaq. Before the Big Shaq character, he was also known as Dr. Ofori in his mockumentary, 'SWIL (Somewhere in London)'. It was through his comedic online skits that he was able to gather a following. After doing a bit of research into his life and his background, it made sense to me why he has achieved so much recently.

In an interview with Tech Insider, we get to see the real Michael talk about life before the fame. In his interview, he mentions how his journey to where he is right now was not smooth sailing. He had to overcome barriers of fear, patterns of inconsistency, believing in himself and his work and also believing that he was going to be successful. Is this not a battle we all face? In the process to get to where we want to, we will have to overcome personal obstacles and self-limiting beliefs, which I talked about in chapter seven.

The pivotal point in Michaels life came in 2015 when he was working part-time at a telephone company. At this point, he had been spending time alone, finding himself and was on the journey to discovering his creative side. Life happened and he lost a very good friend of his to suicide. His friend had a big impact in his life and was actually the one who helped to film one of his YouTube sketches. The loss of his friend, who he looked up to, made him realise, in his words, 'There is more to life than this'. This spurred him to start creating his content which eventually led to his mockumentary, 'SWIL', and his character, 'Big Shaq'. Michael's story is an inspiring one. One where he did not allow his fears to hinder his process, a story where he turned his pain into purpose and when life gave him lemons, he made lemonade!

THE PROCESS

When life gives you lemons, what do you do?

You make lemonade! In your process to become the best version of yourself, you will face challenges. I will label your challenges as 'lemons'. The purpose of the process is to reach the desired end or outcome – This can be called 'lemonade'. In this section, I will be guiding you on a tutorial on how to make lemonade – this will be helpful as a guide on what to do when the lemons of life pop out of nowhere.

Lemons = Challenges of life

Lemonade = The outcome of your challenges

How to make lemonade.

Cut lemons in half and juice through strainer.

I mentioned above how lemons represent the challenges of life and in this scenario, the strainer is your mind. Cutting lemons in half and juicing through a strainer, represents you breaking down your problems and processing your emotions. To process your emotions, you should ask yourself questions.

How am I feeling?

Am I feeling happy?

Am I feeling sad?

By asking yourself these questions it will help you to process your emotions because most times, it is hard to see the truth about a situation when your emotions are clouded. Getting clarity on your emotions will help you handle the challenges of life better!

Create a sugar solution

You create your sugar solution by adding sugar (to your taste) to water and stirring it. In this scenario, this represents how you react to the problems of life. When faced with a challenge that is likely to make you flare up emotionally, my advice to you is to not react to that situation immediately. For example, your colleague keeps belittling everything you do at work and you know you are in a process which involves not lashing out and having composure, my advice to you would be to leave that situation alone. If you need to take a break, do so!

When back in a calm state, you can then address the situation in a calm and orderly manner making it clear to your colleague that you do not appreciate the way they belittle you. The same applies if you are feeling sad, do the opposite! Leave that situation alone, get distracted from it and come back when you are in the right state to get the best outcome and this is you creating a sugar solution.

Combine sugar solution and lemon juice which makes lemonade!

This final step is only possible when you have extracted the lemon juice and created your sugar solution. This means you will have processed your emotions and controlled your reactions to respond in the appropriate manner to that challenge of life. The result is lemonade – a happy stress-free life. You cannot control the amount and frequency of challenges you get in the process, but what you can control is how you process and react to it.

Always remember that when life gives you lemons, you make lemonade!

The Purpose behind the Pain

Michael Dappah was able to turn his pain into purpose. He was able to use that tragic moment to change the trajectory of his life. Part of the process is discovering that area of your life that brings you pain, turning it around, and using it to push you to become the best version of yourself.

There is a purpose behind every pain you went through or are currently going through. As a firm believer in God, I believe that everything happens for a reason and you can either choose to be a victim and be overcome by your pain or you can decide to be a victor by turning your pain into purpose. Pastor John Gray, in one of his sermons, talked about the purpose behind pain. He mentioned that pain births growth depending on your perspective. We can either see the problem behind the pain, the product behind the pain or the power being the pain – this is all down to your perspective.

Many people would rather dwell on how their father walked out on them or how they had to look after themselves from a young age due to irresponsible parents. They would dwell on this in self-pity expecting someone to magically walk into their life and save them. Other people may acknowledge the pain they went through being bullied as a child and realise that this does not have to define them. By doing this, they decide to work on themselves and forget the things of old – in other words, they use their pain to commit to a higher purpose.

The final type of people are those who recognise that the pain they went through had to happen so they could get to where they are now. They are the type that take a look back at their lives and are amazed because everything makes sense. These could be people that may have been abused as a child and gone through a tough childhood, but rather than covering themselves in self-pity, they shift their perspective and discover the power behind their pain. Through the power behind their pain, they use it to start an organization that raises awareness on child abuse. Eventually, this organization grows and impacts thousands of lives – isn't this better than the one who lived through their pain in self-pity? I urge you to recognise the power behind your pain and in your process, let it drive you to purpose and a fulfilled life.

Using your pain in the right way can be instrumental to that fulfilled life you have always wanted.

Do not compare your process to others

It is very important to note that your process will not be the same as everyone else's, so I urge you to not fall into the trap of self-comparison in the process. It can be very easy to compare where you are now to where your friends may be. Process means motion, on the way, headed to a destination and as long you are moving in the right direction, that is all that matters.

To illustrate, I will use the motorway as an analogy for the process of getting to your desired end. The motorway consists of many different cars with different capacities all headed to various destinations. There are usually three lanes which include the slow left lane, the middle overtaking lane, and the right fast lane. Each lane has a different meaning to everyone on the motorway. Some are on the slow lane, overtaking lane, or some are in a haste in the fast lane. Is this not how the process is? Your process may involve you being in the slow lane but making steady, constant progress, while your friend may be in the fast lane headed to their desired destination.

What is really important, whilst on the motorway, (the process) is focus. The one who is in focus is guaranteed to arrive at their destination safely and in due time. However, the one who keeps looking to the right or left, watching others pass by may end up putting themselves at risk of an accident. The one who is focused is powerful, so I encourage you to put all your efforts and energy into where you're going. Trust the process and know through applying the principles mentioned in this book, you will end up right where you are meant to be when you are meant to be there.

Focus on you and I can assure you, your process will be a success!

About the Author

Timi Adeyemo is an emerging author, public speaker, and entrepreneur who calls England home. As an award-winning speaker, he has had the opportunity to attend an array of speaking engagements, motivating individuals from all walks of life.

Timi's affinity for writing began from an early age. When he was 13, his mini story was published in a young writers' book entitled "Tales from the South" and was selected in a young writers creative writing competition back in 2011. His avid interest in personal development piqued when he was a rugby player, and from 13 to 18, he leveraged various motivation methods to improve both his athletic ability and mindset.

Timi then went off to university, where he truly discovered the mind's infinite power. Prior to this pivotal moment, he was never one to strive for the best because he didn't believe in himself fully. The ultimate shift in his overall mindset came while listening to Dr. Myles Munroe talk about ground breaking success principles. It's at that time when he truly internalized one simple yet profound fact: You can alter your viewpoints by **believing** you can. A few other huge influences along his journey have been Bishop TD Jakes, Eric Thomas, and Hal Elrod. It is these inspirational individuals and his change in mindset that enabled him to establish multiple entrepreneurial ventures.

Today, as a firm believer in the power of the mind, Timi

Adeyemo is on a lifelong mission to inspire people to harness their infinite potential so they can alter their perceptions and ultimately transform their entire lives. His first-hand experiences have shaped that vision, and he will stop at nothing to help others become their best versions. To find out more about the author and this book, please visit Timi's website at www.theprocess.info

Book Timi to Speak

'Timi is a principled and inspiring speaker. He speaks with simplicity and great insight. His particular message to millennials is needed more than ever before but also thought provoking to others'.

Christine Bamigbola
President, Windsor Speakers 2018/2019
Director, Public Speaking & Coaching Academy.

'Timi is a dynamic and engaging speaker who has an ability to connect with his audience throughout his talk. An inspirational speaker that will keep you on the edge of your seat right from the start'.

Leela Bassi
International Keynote Speaker,
Above & Beyond Resilience

'Becoming the best version of yourself that you can is not simple, but Timi makes it easy. He writes and speaks with empathy, clarity, and passion. He'll soon have you on your journey to being the best version of you that you can be'.

Clinton Wingrove,
Principal Consultant,
Clinton HR Ltd

To contact Timi about speaking at your event, school, university or corporate firm, visit www.theprocess.info

To connect with Timi, follow @Timispeaks on Social Media

Notes

[1] Jean M. Twenge, PhD. 2007. *Generation Me: Why Today's Young Americans Are More Confident, Assertive, Entitled-and More Miserable Than Ever Before.* Free Press.

[2] Goleman, Daniel. 1996. *Emotional Intelligence: Why it can matter more than ID.* London: Bloomsbury Publishing Plc.

[3] Mischel, Walter. 2014. *The Marshmallow Test: Mastering Self-Control.* Little, Brown and Company.

[4] Gates, Philip. 2017. *Impatience 'costing people £2000 a year'.* October 6. https://www.insider.co.uk/news/financial-services-compensation-scheme-survey-11292387.

[5] Ceccoli, Velleda C. 2014. 'ON PASSION: and the feeling of intensity'. *Velleda C. Ceccoli Ph.D.* August 12. http://drceccoli.com/2014/08/on-passion-and-the-feeling-of-intensity/.

[6] Peat, Jack. 2018. *Millennials 'Spend 10 hours a week on dating apps'.* January 23. https://www.independent.co.uk/life-style/dating-apps-millenials-10-hours-per-week-tinder-bumble-romance-love-a8174006.html.

[7] Hosie, Rachel. 2018. *Single people to spend 96 millions hours...* January 29. https://www.independent.co.uk/life-style/love-sex/single-people-dating-costs-spending-apps-hours-relationships-online-drinks-meals-bad-dates-a8183391.html#gallery.

[8] Watson, William. 2015. *In defense of humanity's oldest institution.* Colorado, Lakewood. http://www.ccu.edu/centennial/2015/09/in-defense-of-humanitys-oldest-institution/.

Printed in April 2022
by Rotomail Italia S.p.A., Vignate (MI) - Italy